Brunella Longo

The Neglected Librarian

Seven articles

about cataloguing big data

2010-2011

London

Online Data Assessment

2017

British Library Cataloguing-in-Publication Data:

A catalogue record for this book is available from the British Library

www.bl.uk

Paperback First edition 2017 ISBN 978-0-9932214-3-9

Ebook PDF / Kindle First edition 2020 ISBN 978-0-99322-14-4-6

© Maria Brunella Longo 2017, 2020

London

Online Data Assessment

email: oda@brunellalongo.co.uk

Contents

Preface *5*

1 What's in a Title Proper? About the future of cataloguing *6*

2 After MARC and beyond: what has to be done in LMSs? *8*

3 The nature of authority control work after divorce from cataloguing *10*

4 How do you name things when the "category issue" is a big business? *13*

5 Towards wikified versions of classification schemes? *15*

6 Science governance may require expansive classifications *17*

7 Cataloguing people (and their relationships) *21*

Definitions *22*

Appendix: In the Cloud *23*

To my mum

Preface

Between 2010 and 2011 I wrote seven articles for an online blog under the title *Brublog: a blog about cataloguing and more*. I published it at first on my website and then on various blogs platforms. The articles were also anticipated or further discussed within digital forums (see the Appendix "In the Cloud" for a list of the public web places where I shared such contents, linked from my own website at the time).

With *Brublog* I had the ambition to reach out potential customers in academic institutions, global organisations and the public sector: these were the groups I would advice about digital developments and the appropriate policies for the evolution of what is the most important asset of any library and data collection, the catalog. To that extent, I redefined *cataloguing* as an asset management activity that could and should be performed in any sector, subject to appropriate information governance.

Writing a blog seemed a good way to engage with a wide global audience and start a conversation about the future of any type of cataloguing process in libraries as well as in other organisations (archives, museums, accounting firms and potentially any company). In fact, the existence of this process is deeply rooted in the ways in which any organisation creates or acquires, keeps and shares records, either through standardised or through proprietary procedures.

Other essential keywords would have been datasets, information retrieval, project, workforce optimisation technologies, vendors and more: for each, I wrote and shared essential definitions that would possibly cause more than few traditionalists to raise an eyebrow. The simple choice of these words revealed that my cultural approach was surely, though quite unintentionally, crushing disciplinary boundaries and allow cross-fertilisation or horizontal innovations to happen among different fields of professional practices, with the result of uncertain scenarios becoming visible.

After few months *Brublog* had attracted innumerable copycats and repeated malicious hacking and denial of service attacks to my website so that it turned out very demanding for me to just keep it online. I decided to divert my energies towards more infrastructural, engineering and organisational aspects of digital environments and the following year promoted a data project management methodology and started my online and printed magazine on change management, *icm²re*.

Brublog articles are republished here with little editing. They may be judged dull or useless, forgotten forever or recognised as the first stepping stones of a big data era in which human beings are still needed to facilitate freedom of expression as well as understanding, preservation and management of data and information at any stage.

11 March 2017

What's in a Title Proper? About the future of cataloguing

This is an edited version of a message I posted on Monday 11 October 2010 on a Mailing List (DC-RDA). I think it can be usefully shared more openly.

It is all about an apparently pitiful innovation introduced by the new Resource Description and Access Cataloguing standard. That highlighted how hilly and complex, but at the same time creative and intellectually interesting, can be for librarians-cataloguers the introduction of new technology-based practices in what is now an internationalized, global, widely participated "cross community metadata landscape".

For more than forty years librarians-cataloguers have been dealing with the concept of "Title Proper" as the main entry point to bibliographic data produced in a static and fixed format, ideal for control and preservation of our cultural heritage goods. Forget it.

Today, library data are seen to gradually become more and more flexible and shareable as "linked data" in the open Web, as datasets, to feed and foster information and research processes deeply interrelated with commercial interests and with the dynamics, the pressure and the politics of the creative industries.

Cataloguing is not anymore a simple and rigid process managed in a highly hierarchical way by National Authorities of the Library World. On the contrary, it is evolving towards a "Many ways together" model, truly internationalised and governed, not without uncertainty and contradictions, by consensus.

Authority control with regard to qualified headings and identifiers is still important but is not enough to assure quality of catalogues. In this new open data environment, cataloguing has become a complex, mature activity that requires sophisticated approaches, great scoping, exceptional focus on information, research or preservation needs of diverse audiences. It demands portfolio, programme and project management - more than good practices managed for decades with the same people. It requires understanding of legal and records management requirements - and probably much more. It is not just how good you are at cataloguing rules learned through your librarianship school or how good you are at managing cataloguers, copy-cataloguing services and paraprofessionals on a job rotation basis.

Thus, let's go back to the pitiful question. The Title Proper of a work can be linked to many other titles of the same work and to the titles of its related expressions and / or manifestations. And one can add a potentially infinite number of parallel titles to a bibliographic record because these are meant to be just variants of the title automatically handled by a software system - simply more "access points" to bibliographic records.

The concept of "main entry" in a catalog simply does not exist anymore in the way it has been conceived and agreed internationally in 1961 - neither in RDA nor in the new international cataloguing principles (and sorry for Michael Gorman, a great librarian that unfortunately was not able to understand the technological scenario we have been heading towards since the early 1990s while he was still stuck on the concept developed during the 1980s).

What we cannot delegate to any software system is the decision about what types of data it makes sense to have in a certain catalog in order to facilitate the discovery of resources - and obviously also their use, reuse and preservation - among a certain type of users. This is why cataloguing is going to be transformed in a process more and more technologically driven.

At the same time, it will become incredibly more discretional and creative than it has been during the past forty years. It was dominated by standardisation and efficiency of the process. It will require more design skills and collaborative contributions, more cultural openness and information policies, more interpretations of contexts and understanding of real usages of data in the next future.

I like the idea of automatic recommendations - data about the usage or search habits of other users (for instance the preferred languages or formats) that help with some displaying, sorting or ranking options, like the Amazon's or LibraryThing's suggestions about similarities; for instance "you may like also...". But I think these usage data cannot substitute cataloguers' editorial control and governance role - also because usage data at present can be easily flawed, and they are not enough reliable neither from a technological nor from a legal point of view.

In an increasingly "open data" scenario, counterbalanced with more data protection, security issues and privacy laws, the user will be required to be increasingly in control of his/her usage data - and in my opinion more likely to appreciate new, transparent, diversified pathways to discover resources than the highly predictable, quite clumsy and obvious "personalised suggestions" easily available at Amazon.

12 October 2010

7

2

After MARC and beyond: what has to be done in LMSs?

This is an extended and edited version of a message I posted on Cilip Linkedin Forum on 31 October 2010.

A question posted on Cilip Linkedin forum by the General Manager of a software company and some pub jokes shared with software developers after a "Mashed librarians" gathering (#Mashspa, Bath, 29 October 2010), made me think that time has come to speed up the pace of new developments in the library management system (LMS) "lab" (and in Google lab too).

As far as I know tests with RDA (Resource Description and Access, the new standard that should replace AACR2 in several Countries) will end in one year and only at that point it will be realistic to prepare a scenario / strategy from the perspective of a LMS provider, in my opinion.

At any rate, I have found the question very appropriate: this is the right time to start rethinking the whole matter and may be expanding the horizon beyond blurring distinctions among media types. In fact, also other segments of the software industry traditionally used for managing data of educational resources, audiovisuals, grey literature, company files, etc have been challenged by the new demand of data integration and sharing in open formats. In the public and educational sectors we should think about LMS features in terms of "Library and Learning Management Systems", truly beyond the organisational space of the library and its traditional workflows.

With regard to MARC, it is therefore clearly impossible for a LMS vendor to make any further effort on it worthwhile for the future - that does not mean at all it is not important anymore in current practices, as many librarians and copy-services managers could confirm. Just it is inevitably not strategic anymore to invest in it (*"MARC is a niche data communication format approaching the end of its life cycle"*, finally stated an OCLC Research report in March 2010, ten years later the acknowledgement of this evidence by the Library of Congress that decided to abandon its legacy system in 2000).

Design of future cataloguing needs to be pretty much more diversified and contextual than it is required at present. It will be increasingly driven by actual user needs more than by abstract functions or highly structured practices. It will be aimed at delivering of library data as metadata in a plurality of formats and possible re-uses of bibliographic information in an "open data" space, where data, metadata, *paradata* and interpretations of data usages will inevitably co-exist.

Therefore, I see two ways to go ahead on this purpose of rethinking the LMS functions. These may be profitably integrated at some point: the first way is top down and consists in picking up successful features currently available within other information systems and search products and propagate them within one's own LMS. The second is bottom up: start analysing and designing the new system from data usages. Beyond libraries' boundaries, cases in metadata management in the private sectors could also be useful in that: they show how focussing at first on the interactions between the process and the people, not the data or the formats, can be successful to find consensus on technical formats too. Dozens of cases in logistics, finance, transports have implemented new extranets EDI and procurement systems that simply could have not been possible without good management of administrative and descriptive metadata. But Amazon or Wal-Mart are not in business to explain how they use their strategic and commercial data to the world, including their competitors, for the sake of interoperability standards.

Simplicity works every time you look at the essential things, not at perfection, and these do not care too much about openness. On the contrary, great sustainable innovations come up when creative minds look at the obvious in new ways, with deep understanding or implicit embedding of common information behaviours habits and patterns. It sounds amazingly surprising to me, for instance, that in the results of many online library catalogs pages (including the ones managed with the newest systems and LMS modules) we still do not show to the user the history of previous searches within the same session nor the visualisation of the entire usage data neither; we do not ask users for permissions to store their data or to re-use them as validated, reviewed, commented, clarified components of their own research processes or for other purposes.

Finally, it seems to me there is a competence gap to be addressed. IT innovations in information management, particularly in the library sector, have been led for years by managers trained in the 1970s on mainframe accountancy systems and then by geeks trained in the 1990s almost exclusively in programming languages and DBMS with little understanding of information retrieval principles and impact on acquisition and sharing of knowledge. The increased use of ITIL, Prince2, Agile and many others project management schemes, methods and recipes during the last ten or fifteen years has been producing brilliant results in efficiency of software developments but mainly outside the library world. A growing community of advanced internet users and passionate geeks is being stimulated to develop ideas, prototypes, gadgets, widgets, applications and whatever with "mashed" data and APIs in order to enlarge the online advertising market and to experiment new creative, commercial and technical possibilities of new businesses with open data. It's not rocket science to note there is a demand for leadership and directions in all these separated fields with a common scope of managing information through cataloguing processes.

01 November 2010

3

The nature of authority control work
after divorce from cataloguing

No work ever to be entered twice at full lenght.
[Antonio Panizzi, 1841]

The results of a Delphi survey among 70 librarians expert of cataloguing are published in the current issue of "Cataloguing and Classification Quarterly" (*A Research Agenda for Cataloging: The CCQ Editorial Board Responds to the Year of Cataloging Research* / by Richard P. Smiraglia. -http://doi.org/aje). I could not be more satisfied as the results go in the direction I have explored myself - see my "CPD-Wiki", page "*A Second look at cataloguing practices*" at [*omissis, the online resource is not available anymore*] - when cataloguing is defined as an active process that includes "external links to bibliographic databases and the semantic web".

Nevertheless, I noticed something a bit odd in that the definition restates the importance of linking descriptions to authority files as part of that active process. Hold on a minute, I said myself. How sad is this story! It sounds like two who had consensually divorced because of fiscal and legal convenience (blaming the girl they illegally fired, forced away from her father and made her appearing as a criminal lover just for the subcultures they needed to feed with advertising revenues, you know), who then found they were both really happier living separate lives and still had lot of common interests, who may now share businesses, networks, second homes and one garage in the city but... now are also required to appear together in the parochial journal? really? for the sake of the "community" and more advertising revenues? And still blaming the girl? Is this fair? Certainly it is not. Fact is they have divorced, no matter the ruses and the fakes, and that is forever.

Then, seriously, I had to admit Smiraglia has that extraordinary quality of provoking constant engagement through humour that was the peculiarity of writing and teaching about cataloguing and classification theories of my mentor Luigi Crocetti. And yet, there are reasons why things are defined in a way or another, named and mentioned... or not.

I did not mention authority work in my own cross-domain definition of cataloguing (one could say 'entrepreneurial', it may be!) because:

1) I have elaborated such definition to investigate applications of cataloguing skills in diverse segments or niches of the information management sector and

2) the definition was meant to "tag" a very small, bit cluttered (ehm, I was about to write *cuttered*), and very personal collection of links to websites, projects and technologies publicly shared at *http://www.connotea.org/user/search/tag/cataloguing* that document currents trends in cataloguing.

Everybody aware of the current state of development of authority control work knows we have entered a period, about fifteen years ago, that constitutes a financially tough but intellectually sparkling moment for cataloguing, probably in a timescale that span more than 150 years.

Global and local initiatives, international standards, parallel projects dealing with diverse technologies and new products as web services are basically reshaping the matter and redefining balances and strategies to be pursued collaboratively with authors, publishers, governments and non governmental organisations.

In any sector interested by web technologies and web services there is an increased need for cataloguing activities: for instance, while I am editing this blog post from an email message that I have catalogued in my personal "to be further shared" folder, I am reminding myself to quote in a paper the excellent categorisation of the types of frauds published by the Action Fraud website at http://actionfraud.org.uk and to browse the new BIC Standard Subject Categories mentioned in the Catalogue & Index Blog at http://communities.cilip.org.uk/blogs/catalogueandindex/default.aspx.

There are reasons why my own definition does include records management, for instance, even if I am not sure there is enough literary warrant for that yet - but I see records management standards, particularly the ones concerning the production of metadata, as key crucial factors for engineering the whole process, for the integrity and consistency of catalogues data shared as linked data through the web, especially if one takes into account the peculiarities of digital curation and preservation (in any sector). My definition refers also to datasets, and so on and so forth. There are reasons for each of these details. But yes, my definition does not mention authority control.

Fact is that more than ten years ago authority work was said to be specific of some libraries' and services' requirements - and not universally needed anymore ("*IFLA goal of universal bibliographic control by way of requiring everyone to use the same form for headings globally is not practical and is no longer necessary*", was the 1998 conclusion of an international working group).

Therefore I think time has come to clearly state in a general cross domain definition of catlaoguing what librarians, indexers, information retrieval experts, linked data guru and other specialists have in common.

I believe authority control work is crucial for the entire information management sector, first of all for information governance reasons. It is crucial these days in contexts that are experimenting new standards for open data spaces: these may make an author invisible in some authority files, perceived as dead in some others, confused with homonyms or misrepresented via intentionally or unintentionally faked results. The last can be part of defamatory and stigmatisation campaigns with serious consequences on the reputation of people, especially independent or young researchers, and are known to be astonishingly under-reported.

So, all in all, I reframed the authority control work and put it in the larger context of information policies and governance of the semantic web where, as far as I can see, there is chance it can be crucial for the design and development, management and implementation of new standards (like http://www.isni.org/) and new identifiers in any sector.

07 December 2010

4

How do you name things when
the "category issue" is a big business?

How do you categorise Internet studies, asked Bill Dutton in his Oxford Internet Institute's Blog? And why those involved in this field seem to underrate this "category issue" - while evidence are being gathered about the fact that massive targeted unethical and illegal activities are increasingly carried out through search engines and social media (that lead to frauds and other serious financial crimes as well as to manipulation of search terms, metadata, connections from social networking sites and consequent alteration of search engines results pages for all sorts of commercial, political and libellous reasons).

I am very interested in the question. These that follow are my answers, originally posted as comments and kindly published in the OII Director's Blog.

In the early '90s, following several years I spent classifying books and other materials for public libraries and for a worldwide advertising agency, I was recruited to become the author of a classification scheme of the global audiovisual sector used by Mr. Berlusconi's group of companies (Fininvest, that then made the TV division Mediaset public), when the definition of the relevant market for advertising in Italy and in Europe was crucial for bringing about a new legislation and allow the development of commercial television. For the next ten years I then researched, shaped and defined taxonomies, architectures and data structures in other broad areas, research fields, market segments such as telecommunications. I also did it in order to design commercial products as a consultant, as a project manager or as an information designer of websites, databases and electronic services. It is a shame but perhaps also a sign of our times that I am now struggling to find work in this area. Why? Has the market and social demand for thinking dropped? How will we engineer the infrastructure of the knowledge economy if those who should profit from it do not have any knowledge of its semantic foundations?

A proper classification or taxonomy of internet studies has not been devised yet because the sector is still considered in its infancy, there is no general academic acceptance of it outside some rare special departments or research centres (like the OII), and "battles for the dominance" of its commercial, legal and governance routes are still going on.

Search the subject "internet" in most of the library catalogs (including, for instance, http://searchbeta.bl.uk/, http://copac.ac.uk , http://library.ox.ac.uk/ just to name few examples of three diverse generations of library management systems) and you recall thousands of books, journals, conference papers. Without any possibility of further categorisation of this impressive quantity of materials it is very hard and time consuming to select and access new resources, make comparisons, find new ideas and theories and perform very basic operations that prelude to any serious advance in studying the field. It seems to me that the interdisciplinary nature of the internet has not been shaped and defined in more manageable chunks, for now, since I started to study this cross-domain sector in the early 1990s.

An interesting exception comes from (still rare) catalogs that facilitate resource discovery in that they apply to traditional bibliographic records new data mining technologies to produce "faceted views" of the results. For instance, searching for internet as subject in http://ncsu.worldcat.org/ gives you about 330,620 items narrowed by 31 diverse "topics". That means the results are automatically aggregated on the ground of disciplinary divisions. Browse them and you may better define a more complex set of multiple words that can represent the specificity of what you are looking for. Besides, these subdivisions of the subject "internet" testify that internet studies represents a truly new cross-domain field that should require novel attention by cataloguers, taxonomists and indexers.

Nevertheless, Bill Dutton's question has first of all a political meaning. I am convinced that internet has become an indispensable utility (like water, energy and the telephone) facing the challenge of unacceptable levels of cybercrime activities and lack of proper global governance. As a new field of academic studies, Internet is exposed to conflicts for public funding among diverse academic disciplines while the regulators and the media moguls are fighting about the definition, the boundaries and even the nature of the internet advertising market, essentially from an antitrust perspective.

I myself started considering internet as a new medium in the 1990s because online advertising seemed to be the main source of revenue for many internet companies and the most relevant business model. But that, from a classification point of view, was a typical mistake known as "classification by attraction". *Nomen est omen*, one could say! As soon as you try to get deeply into the internet taxonomy business you notice that it is simply impossible to contain internet studies within the media sector. Internet is not at all just a "new medium". It contains and delivers at the same time several media and technologies of communication, social spaces, regulatory domains and styles of interaction, learning and relationships, including grey economies areas that cannot stay unregulated any longer if we want to prevent social risks and the expansion of cybercrime activities. All the diverse "facets" of the Internet diamond must inevitably coexist. Hence the political importance of having a shared cross-domain taxonomy that can be an enabling tool for research, governance and policies, an authoritative point of reference for search engines and social networking sites and, last but not least, an essential strategic instrument to speed up effectiveness and progress of internet studies.

05 January 2011

5

Towards "wiki-fied" versions of classification schemes?

This is an extended and edited version of the comments I posted to Prince2:2009
Author Blog *on 10 December 2010 and to the Cilip Cataloguing and Indexing Blog on 17
December 2010.*

I have been impressed by the tidy simple interface of the new BIC Standard Subject
Categories Website (available at http://82.35.102.10/bic_categories) and by its easy of use
but also surprised by some oddities in the subject headings. These clearly reflect
marketing priorities and cultural trends that would be very interesting to see commented
and discussed by experts, end-users, practitioners over time.

For instance, CILIP Cataloguing and Indexing blog published an announcement last
month in which it was said that "mathematicians will be thrilled to see that Bayesian
Inference now has its own category". Oh my God! That is a scoop, I thought.

But I have not been able to find the Bayesian Inference method quoted neither in a
subject headings of the BIC nor in any of its notes or guidelines so far: it has already been
revised? Did I access the wrong site? I would not be surprised to note that Bayesian
Inference has its own category considered the publicity it received during the last year in
many contexts, for instance in the last issue of "Communications of the ACM" or with the
2010 Turing lecture at the IET (given by Bishop, C., 2010 with the suggestive title
Embracing uncertainty: the new machine intelligence. The IET/BCS Turing Lecture, 25
February 2010. Available at http://tv.theiet.org/technology/infopro/turing-2010.cfm).

I remember the method described in the excellent syllabus of my university's
information retrieval course I took in 1992 (and passed *cum laudem* - as my Bliss
classification and cataloguing courses I am pleased to say, but these disciplines have now
become obsolete).

It is a bit sad to note that nothing is really changed since then, from a scientific point
of view. But it is also true that there is more and more alleged bayesian support to
everything requires surveys and polls, comments and thoughts, opinions and inspirational
views by the media, the blogs and the social networks thanks to a huge amounts of data
processed electronically (or better to say crowdsourced) serving multiple scopes and
domains, including public engagement and understanding of science.

I am very curious to see the developments of such a celebration of the method because
so far it can be quoted by the press and it surely supports some decision making processes
adding transparency and evidences of public opinion and common knowledge dynamics,

but it does not seem to be counting when we want to assess any scientific or legal truth. Like authors of paranormal novels, bayesians explorers have never made any scientific discovery though they might have offered to the information available more visibility.

Conversely, innumerable are the examples of major achievements in any STEM field thanks to the intuition of single-minded researchers as well as traditional and systematic R&D processes: for instance, Stephanie Kwolek invented Kevlar, that is commonly used in body armour saving lives of millions, because she decided she wanted to work for DuPont and DuPont financed her for 17 years.

I recently considered some advances in information retrieval techniques from a forensic point of view (see my *Cataloguing the unfindable: mapping cybercrime in information management practices*). It seems to me that there are new promising approaches that could complement or supersede bayesian calculations even in other fields, like budget allocation and science policies, increasing our ability to deal with crowdsourcing findings in an intelligently controlled, productive and risk-aware way (most of the times we completely ignore the way in which other will use what we say in the short as well as in the long term on a rational base but we tend to see analogical relationships, coincidences and cause-effect relationships everywhere in our over-connected, information rich world, often "attracting" meanings in our own context without being aware and without caring at all of their original meanings and functions).

Having said that, I do not think that subject headings related to information retrieval or crowdsourcing technologies have to include references to all the available methods, ranking them and assessing their potential in this or that context - obviously. It is just to say that naming them all, as examples, within scope or definition notes of a classification could be helpful and instructive to any audience of the same scheme and would support more rationale, audited and controlled processes in any STEM project.

Enumerating and making more visible and "connectable" our classes, categories and isolated topics could also facilitate quick and productive collaborative transactions among buyers, cataloguers and other professional preventing errors of judgment, wrong and biased decisions and misunderstanding of others' decisions: inferences that allow completely fabricated realities to take over should be recognised for what they are.

So all in all, I would say that in the future the tidy interfaces could be enriched with more interactivity. Features to collect notes and comments from users can be easily added without any particular software programming effort to any website. It seems to me that information governance strategies and productivity goals justify the systematic, managed and audited, adoption of technologies of collaborations: we could and should have "wiki-fied" versions of any classification scheme or thesaurus as long as we recognise the provenance of any single contribution to our common knowledge spaces.

31 January 2011

6

Science governance may require expansive classifications

This is an extended and edited version of the comments I wrote for the Wellcome Trust's Blog post reviewing the 2010 "Science and Citizenship" Conference, available at http://wellcometrust.wordpress.com/2011/01/05/if-science-were-a-play-would-its-audience-be-the-public/#comment-1690

Science governance and cataloguing practices may appear two fields very far from each other. But they were born together in the XIII Century when scientific knowledge and classification systems shared the assumption of a finite, perfectly and totally knowledgeable single universe.

Then, for many centuries, scientists, merchants and technologists on one side and philosophers and librarians on the other followed diverse routes: the first negotiated their territories, methods and projects with a plurality of social actors (politicians, religious authorities and their audiences); the second were less interested in dialogs and interactions since they were always secured a living by the authorities and they were almost always speaking only with their peers within closed walls -   convents, universities, librarians' schools, public bureaucracies, professional associations.

In a specular opposite way, after so many years, and with the anticipations of small communities of documentalists, information scientists and anomalous librarians (suddenly called "special librarians" and "information officers") who led the way since the early 1910s, science education and classification systems seem now at the beginning of a new common era in which the two fields share the same high levels of uncertainty and awareness about the volatility and extreme mutability of what we call "scientific knowledge".

On top of that, people working in both fields are increasingly pressurised and made in some ways accountable for any action and any decision they make (or not) within the perimeter of interests of a dilated global world of potential stakeholders (that include not only regulators, politicians and the public opinion but also, potentially, single bloggers as well as foreign governments). What does this mean for our open societies fundamental freedoms such as freedom of expression and freedom of enterprise?

Some sort of reductionism and simplification may be needed. Or, in other terms, we should think science governance in very plain terms, as the entire "command and control" system of it should be easily understandable by a teenager, and the entire contents of what is going on within our academic institutions and research organisations should be represented with a single page report. Call it science governance for dummies (with apologies to those who may be offended).

For this simplification to be possible, somebody has to classify what is going on. Not listing, not blogging about, not tagging sentiments for this or that but classifying according to a pre-defined and predictable, constantly evolving scheme of what we see and what we expect to understand from public knowledge over time.

Beneath the coolness of the communication skills and the engagement tools, it seems that the right and continuously changing environment for science communication requires self-perspective, transparency about our own goals and contexts, constant reviews of the workflows and openness about the benefits and the failures we constantly experience dealing with the pressure of new developments and technological changes about almost everything. So, what about starting from who we think we are and what are the achievements or benefits we are looking for?

"*Frame yourself before framing the question*" was my final, shared consideration about science governance in the age of knowledge uncertainties at the end of the interesting Conference I joined last December (Science and Citizenship, organised by the British Council at the Wellcome Collection Conference Centre, 14 and 15 December 2010). That is probably true both for the investigators and communicators on one side and for the audiences of science engagement and education initiatives on the other.

I was very happy to see I was not alone in considering that a line should always be drawn between publicity and education, surveys of the general public and the attitudes of selected opinion leaders' collected for fundraising or public policy reasons - even though media experts and communication specialists can find the issue quite naive these days. In fact, from their legitimate though cynical point of view, the more ambivalent and confused is the field, the better seems the market for creativity, communication and advertising or educational services that may include disambiguation and clarification of statements among the projects' outcomes. But, for how long? would you really have time to cheer the tricks of your primary school teachers while you are looking for your first job or when you try to reckon your pension annuities? There is something that defines us in relation to our own knowledge and that is our learning curve: we learn and change our mind for the entire duration of our life.

Clarity should be settled at the beginning of science communication projects: it is a methodological assumption that makes any research question a valid and manageable business case over time. If we want to promote the demand of science education we have to understand what stimulates people to long-life learning and continuous professional development in their contexts, beyond any emotional or instrumental endorsement of this or that campaign. And we should always understand what motivates people to share what they *already* know if we want to collect reliable science policies insight (including both factual data and beliefs) from reliable sources.

Last year I attended another interesting conference that stretched the point of interpretations of assumptions and reliability of outcomes along the science communication spectrum (Cancer Research: lost in translation? A half day conference organised in partnership by the British Library and the NCRI Informatics Initiative, British Library Conference Center 19th January 2010). In this occasion, some critical factors attracted many considerations from the participants, like the need for translation strategies (how to turn discoveries into clinical benefits while maintaining investments into basic research) and patients engagement strategies (how to convince patients that involvement in clinical trials is beneficial for them as well as for society?).

What it seemed clear to me, thanks to both conferences' debates and talks, was that there is no difference between communication or translation projects with regard to the need of programme and project management methodologies often underestimated by scientists and public officers. Either in communication or in translation, one may have exactly the same processes and related problems to deal with, the differences being originated only by the people and the rules of the game in a specific context: governance, assurance and data protection should be defined within a common framework that should be transparent and evolve and change dynamically, accordingly to uses and evidences of research, remaining consistent and frictionless over time.

The last point was in some ways at the centre of several informal talks during the 'Science and citizenship' conference, with regard to constraints determined by sharing of and access to personal data.

Internet and the digital representations we exchange through online services create glass houses shared among diverse contexts that we are often not at all prepared to manage or take care of for the rest of our lives. Basically, we suddenly realise that our data are out of our own control. Even if you can say 'well, I have nothing to hide' fact is that you do not know what may happen to your data in fifteen years time, how such data may be exchanged, mangled, mixed, interpreted, reported or abused. Infinite usages, re-uses and unfortunately also ruses may happen that could create trouble to your identity, work, family life, financials etc.

Sometimes the threats originate from real physical crimes reported in (and / or distorted by) local newspapers. In other circumstances abuses may be symbolic or fabricated (e.g. through virtual worlds and games environments, without you even being aware of that). Your data may get stolen from a public database or your health records falsified or a photo showing you acting as a human bird in an artistic video can simply be the apparently "innocent" first act of a long chain of unintended little abuses that ends with very serious stigmatisation and defamatory issues, complicating the identification of liabilities and responsibilities among groups of people belonging to diverse contexts, communities, cultures and legal environments.

In the XIX Century, before the decimal classifications took over any other scheme with their excellent simplicity and the predictability of their notations, Charles Cutter wrote an "expansive classification"essay   that, if widely implemented, might have radically changed the way in which we manage bibliographic classifications as well as the pace or rhythm of changes, substitutions and disposals of libraries' collections. In fact, Cutter system was based on the idea of a knowledge life-cycle, a concept further developed by Max Boisot many decades later: everything in the public domain (what we implicit consider public knowledge if not common sense) starts as simple statements, it can become very complicated thanks to human interactions and exchanges until at a certain point collapses into the end of a "knowledge cycle". That is the stage when something that was once upon a time acceptable or even fashionable - think about smoking or talking over the phone while driving for instance - suddenly seems to many just appalling nonsense.

The expansive classification imagined by Cutter would have necessarily required constant tuning and alignment with the consistency of the classified collections, it had long notations and it was unfortunately considered too fast by the... lazy and slow librarians (beware humour in the previous sentence!).

Although the idea of incorporating the mutability of knowledge over time in the notation influenced both the classifications' and the subject headings fields, and I believe it is in its essence an extraordinary modern principle we will re-discover in search of "real time analytics" assurance requirements - Cutter expansive classification was abandoned and it is quite rare that even PhD students in librarianship know it .

We may require now something similar to Cutter's expansive classification for science governance as well as for cataloguing and classification practices: rules must become extremely flexible and simple but they should stay inspired by strong principles that remain clearly constant over time, in spite of climate changes, technological bargains and the data, businesses or collections (in)consistencies.

The project manager could say they always have to scale nicely.

15 February 2011

7

Cataloguing people (and their relationships)

In the last two months for personal reasons I had to search for, access and deal with data related to housing, finance and work matters.

Nothing more real than these practical matters could have stimulated my sensitiveness to emphasise in several occasions (face to face meetings as well as online discussions) the importance of identifiers, standards, assurance and good data management policies and behaviours in order to deal with both personal and factual data in a productive and profitable manner.

But... I had almost no time to update this blog and to indulge in sharing further thoughts in writings. When I was finally about to blog some ideas and references to current conferences and debates, I discovered that previous blogposts had become unaccessible to those not yet registered as members of the ResearchGate platform.

So, I spent at least a couple of hours to create alternatives ways to access previous articles, that I had never intended to be available behind a firewall or authentication system, instead of writing a new one: an archived version of this blog is now available through Blogspot and a printable PDF version is published through my own website.

But I have also had the opportunity to read and read again what I had already written (that is quite rare because we collectively spend more time writing than reading ours or others' blogs). And I discovered that I have already expressed (and even secured the access to, now) reflections about the future of cataloguing that have huge impact on the way in which we identify, monitor and trace people activities and relationships over time in many fields of bibliographic and factual data management.

I feel the goal of this Blog is now completed and what has not been said or specified or commented yet is... better to stay untold for now, and it will be shared another time.

11 April 2011

Definitions

Cataloguing

Any practice and standard used to design, produce, maintain and allow online public access to any type of descriptive and subject catalog, including metadata and linked data, in any Country.

Information governance

Strategies, principles, policies, coded behaviours, quality assurance requirements, compliance to existing law and by-laws and auditing of data and information management in any sector, market or professional practice (including cataloguing and knowledge collection, representation and diffusion).

Open access

The expression is used here in its widest acceptation, including institutional repositories, open archives, open data, OAI-PMH and may be also extended to cover some aspects of open source software (Content management systems and other platforms that allow the design, production, delivery and user monitoring of open access journals).

Project

Any type of temporary endeavour aimed at research and development, design and implementation of digital libraries and related new curatorial practices.

Vendor

Any primary or secondary source of information, with disregard for its original or prevalent business model, discipline or sector. Basically, almost any provider of "digital stuff" identifiable as a stable organisation can be a vendor.

WOT

Workforce Optimization Technologies include Intranet platforms, technologies of collaboration, e-learning / e-coaching software, wikis for business and research projects, project management and events management applications.

Appendix

In the Cloud: Fragments of Brunella Longo's online conversations 2010-2011

When	Where	What	Why
28/3/2011	LIS-Law and UKeIG Mailing lists	Brown's Report review by Stefan Collini	Letter to the London Review of Books about the pros and cons of SERVqual approach to customer satisfaction measurements in Higher Education.
18/3/2011	DC-RDA Mailing list	The "actual" RDA	Contribution to the debate about the future of cataloguing with regard to projects and implementation of the new Resource Description and Access standard.
4/2/2011	LIS-Law and UKeIG Mailing lists	Sharing knowledge	To share a position about the need to constantly review and update communication policies for information management and information problem solving.
31/01/2011	Wellcome Trust Blog	Public engagement with science	Some reflections shared at the Science and Citizenship Conference attended in December 2010 about public engagement policies and science governance. Extendend version: Brublog, 15/2/2011
24/12/2010	LIS-UKBIBS and MARC Forum	MARBI papers available for review	To answer a question raised since 2007 by the Online Audiovisual Catalogers group with regard to the need of a new subfield in MARC 21 bibliographic standard - that can be accommodated through RDA / library linked data standards and participatory cataloguing processes. Debate continued on MARC list at http://bit.ly/marcarchives.
21/12/2010	Phil Bradley's weblog	Net neutrality and cybercrime	To remind the importance of new approaches needed to fight cybercrime.
18/12/2010	Oxford Internet Institute Blogs	Internet Studies Taxonomy	To engage myself in conversation with the internet researchers community and reinforce the statement that a cross-domain, interdisciplinary classification of internet studies is needed - independently from the media industry interests.

When	Where	What	Why
17/12/2010	Catalogue and Index Blog	BIC subject categories	To engage myself in conversation with the C&I group community about: use of bayesian inference, scope and definition notes within web versions of subjects headings and classification schemes.
10/12/2010	Prince2:2009 Author Blog	Review of the year at the Institute of Directors (IOD)	To confirm the importance of data and information management in managing uncertainty and risks in programmes and projects.
20/11/2010	Oxford Internet Surveys Blog	Internet usage	To share findings from my 1990s research projects such as those about the "net disposable time" concept and state the need to discover new categories to investigate internet behaviours.
26/10/2010	British Library Podcasts - Talks, Discussions and Interviews	Is the physical library a redundant resource?	To express an alternative view about the political discourse that pushes for a fictitious conflict among diverse generations of librarians dealing with digital innovations. A metacomment about the comment expressed during the debate is available here as podcast (4 min, 1.9 MB). See also Eight days diary, 3/11/2010 (PDF).
21/10/2010	Harvard Business Review	Information management	To amplify a reflection about knowledge gathering through surveys and crowd-sourcing techniques. These are in my opinion brilliant engagement and promotional tools, the reliability of which is overrated from an information management point of view.
18/10/2010	OCLC Lorcan Dempsey's Blog	Metadata and Google rankings	To re-state and promote the use of metadata for resource discovery and re-design of cataloguing practices I wrote about in a blog post (What's in a Title Proper. About the future of cataloguing, 12/10/2010).
03/10/2010	Catalogue and Index Blog	Future of cataloguing	To re-state that the future of cataloguing is "many ways together" with a plurality of technical standards and machine-interoperable solutions in place, sharing strong common information policies, data and records management governance.

When	Where	What	Why
08/09/2010	Intute Blog	Information services	To amplify a reflection about the forthcoming closure of Intute and to share my vision of innovation in the information services / information literacy field, mostly influenced by Patrice Flichy's theory of innovation (*L'innovation technique*. Paris, 1995).
15/08/2010	Slate.com	Inception interpretations	Opportunity to share some thoughts about the rhetoric of collectivism that I see as an obstacle to effective participation in digital environments.
05/08/2010	Phil Bradley's weblog	Google Wave	Expression of concern about the impact of poor design on user experience and quality of web search interfaces.
03/08/2010	Hadley Beeman's Posterous Blog	A "crowdsourcing metadata" project?	To engage myself in conversation with the Open data community.